EAST CORNWALL
— in the —
OLD DAYS

Joy Wilson

BOSSINEY BOOKS

First published in 1988 by
Bossiney Books
St Teath, Bodmin, Cornwall.

Typeset and Printed by
Clowes Book Printers
St Columb, Cornwall.

Front cover tinted by Maggie
Ginger: An A. E. Raddy
photograph – delivering the
bread in Polperro.
Back cover: Fowey Harbour in
July 1901. The five-masted
schooner *Rebecca Palmer* of
Bristol, the first sailing ship of
her size to cross the Atlantic
and the largest ever to moor in
the Fowey River.

Acknowledgments

I would like to thank the following people who have helped me
with information or the generous loan of photographs: Mike
Bevan, Fowey Museum Project; Bodmin Museum; Gareth
Bullen; Mr and Mrs R. Butson; Lady Carew Pole; Mike Coath;
ECC International; Bill Hopkins, London Postcard Shop;
Mr Lassam, Lacock Abbey Collection; Liskeard Museum;
Lostwithiel Museum; P. Manning, Audio-Visual Archives; Roger
Penhallurick, Royal Institution of Cornwall; Tom Raddy and
Rex Raddy; John Rapson; Kevin Reilly; Saltash Library;
Professor Charles Thomas; Mrs Searle, Torpoint Library;
Muriel Vosper; Richard Carew Pole; The Courtauld Institute
Picture Library; and The National Trust.

About the Author and the Book

Joy Wilson was born and bred in Liverpool in the pre-Beatle era. She was at school at Merchant Taylors' and then spent four years at Trinity College, Dublin, reading French and English Literature. A year in France teaching was followed by a few months in Leicester where she met Colin, her writer husband.

She worked as a Librarian in London and then a year after *The Outsider* was published in 1956 they moved to Cornwall – for six months they thought – but they've been here ever since, making their home in Gorran.

Joy made her debut for Bossiney with a chapter in *Meals for All Seasons,* and then in 1985 contributed to *Westcountry Mysteries.*

In 1986 she made a major contribution to the Bossiney list: *Around St Austell Bay,* the author's words accompanied by a wealth of old photographs and picture postcards.

Now in *East Cornwall in the Old Days* she again skilfully combines text and old pictures. Torpoint and Saltash, Liskeard and Callington, Looe and Polperro are only some of her destinations on this nostalgic journey. Of our debt to the old photographers, Joy Wilson reflects that in their time they 'found their subjects in East Cornwall with the scenery constantly changing in the clear light, its ancient fishing ports and historic inland towns, and the faces of the local people too. Turn the pages to see the record they have left us of what they saw. I hope that their pictures, linked to the varied stories of the past that they evoke, and the details captured in some of the old postcard views may provide for you, as they do for me, a fascinating, if fragmented, mirror of past times in this part of Cornwall.'

EAST CORNWALL in the OLD DAYS

The Devil, I am told by a Saltash lady, stoutly refused ever to cross the Tamar into Cornwall. Perched high on Devil's Point on the Plymouth side and eyeing the green rolling hills of the east Cornish landscape he was deterred by a warning. On such a visit, he was told, there was definite risk that he might become an unwilling and pepper ingredient in a Cornish pasty.

So Cornwall has remained the land of Saints and this beautiful eastern corner of it with the small ancient ports of Saltash and Looe and Fowey has always been the gateway into the county. Until Isambard Kingdom Brunel completed the great railway bridge across the Tamar, East Cornwall, from Bodmin on the fringe of the moor to Lostwithiel and Liskeard to Callington on the slope of Kit Hill, to Saltash and the fishing ports of the coast, remained to travellers remote and mysterious place. Cornish people living here were spoken of as 'pleasant primitives'.

Before the railway brought great changes, the writer Wilkie Collins described this part of Cornwall as the 'most untrodden ground in England' that he could select for a walking tour. The old photographs and postcards of all these places assembled in this book,

FAR RIGHT *Polperro harbour in earlier days.*

RIGHT *Brunel's railway bridge across the River Tamar at Saltash.*

ABOVE Nets being mended at Fowey, a never-ending job, but they were not made in Fowey. They came from Brixham and were very expensive to replace.

think, reflect something of the transformation that has taken place since that time.

Even as late as the 1950s, looking across the wide river towards the Cornish shore, the waters of the Tamar remained a formidable barrier, an age old defence. No road bridge then crossed its lower reaches. Instead, there was an impatient wait on the Devonport bank, then a slow passage across on the loaded ferry with the clanking chains that helped it to resist the seaward pull of the tide.

For the pedestrian that I was then, the fare was a modest penny. Landing at Torpoint with the steep grid pattern of streets we took the old switchback road that skirted the cliffs of the indented East Cornish coastline. It was an arduous but rewarding route over the hills to Looe and on to Polperro and Fowey. There were few crowds even in summer then and something of the old way of life that centred around these ancient harbours still remained.

Today in high summer over the new Tamar road bridge and along the remodelled main roads a tide of traffic hurtles towards the East Cornish coast and these fishing ports. From a speeding car on a by-pass that skirts Saltash or Liskeard or Callington, there seems little to see of these inland towns, or to discover about their ancient streets and the people who lived there once.

But when I was assembling the photographs and pictures for this book, I wandered on foot all around these towns of East Cornwall hoping to find out how much of what had once attracted the eye of the photographer still exists today. Exploring a side street, or looking up at first floor façades above the uniform shopfronts of our time, it was possible to find much that had remained unchanged, and the local residents I met en route often had stories to tell that brought the past to life.

I abandoned the blinkers of main road travel and turned on to the winding roads crossing the green hinterland between the high

RIGHT An early comic postcard.

moorland and the sea. I found that signposts were few and often indicated place-names with a hint of oddity. Merrymeet and Wiggle, Catchfrench and Finnygook, Crafthole, Portwrinkle and Doddycross; all were strange English versions of Cornish originals that reflected the many 'foreign' incursions of the past.

Frequently disoriented in a confusing network of high stone hedges, I found that a turn in a steep lane that was once a pack-horse track might reveal an old Celtic cross, a prehistoric stone circle or a broken avenue of gnarled old beech trees; undiscovered except by a traveller with time to wander.

On a sunlit day with a hint of rain in the air, standing on the cliffs of the Dodman near my home, I can see the long outline of the East

OVERLEAF *Caffa Mill Pill in Fowey in 1900 showing Heller's shipwrights' Yard. Rickard's Stores and sailmakers' loft are on the left.*

7

ABOVE On Looe Bridge, Tom Raddy, the photographer's son, waits with his new bike behind the charabanc carrying a Wesleyan outing in the 1920s. Petrol cans are carried on the running board.

Cornish coast across the bay. White cottages of Polruan climbing the headland, long sandy bays, the Looe estuary and beyond, the slatey promontory of Rame with its hermit's chapel watching over all. They emerge with sudden startling clarity from the usual sea-haze.

Walk a mile or two inland and on the far off skyline is sombre Kit Hill and Caradon encircled with the chimneys of the deserted mines. The Fowey and Looe rivers, the Lynher and the Tamar shaped this landscape and the towns of Lostwithiel and Fowey, Looe and Saltash are all built on the banks of the rivers that brought them trade. Bodmin town and Liskeard are older still; at the heart of each is an ancient Celtic holy well.

All these places and especially the harbours of the coast attracted the photographers whose work is found in these pages. A magnifying glass can reveal details; the graceful design of the gas lamps that once lit Bodmin's Fore Street, the cut of a silk dress worn in Liskeard in 1910, an old woman's threadbare shawl, or a sedate beach party at Looe.

Some themes recur; occasionally, in the message written on the back of a postcard, the First World War; tea-gardens as a destination for an outing; and the almost forgotten ritual of afternoon tea. There are faint traces of past smuggling exploits and the constant struggle to wrest a living from the sea. In this part of Cornwall the French seem to have earned a certain historic unpopularity, while with some cards the unique flavour of Cornish humour emerges too.

The earliest photographer known in Liskeard was a woman who advertised in a local directory, but none of her pioneer work exists today. In the 1890s John Henry Coath set up his business as a professional photographer in a gilder's premises in Liskeard's Lower Lux Street. Later he was able to build a studio of his own and in time two of his sons, Claude and Charles, worked with him as photographers too and the creative quality of all of their work became renowned.

Alfred Ernest Raddy started in life as a postman but, discovering his true talent, he became the first professional photographer of Polperro and Looe. In an old Elizabethan house in Looe's Fore Street he established the photographic business in the early 1900s that continues to be run by his descendants today. Outside the wide old door can still be seen the hitching ring for the pony and trap that he used for photographic excursions or an occasional postal round.

BELOW Photographer Herbert Hughes at work on the Banjo pier at Looe with his friends capturing local boys at play.

ABOVE An early beachcombing scene.

In these early days the professional photographer's art was quite hard work. Heavy bellows cameras and tripods to move around, film washing by hand in cold water in the early morning, the chemicals hard on the skin, while in the studio unruffled politeness to the occasional cantankerous client would be required. Glass negatives mostly used then were fragile and we are lucky to have those that survive today. As a First World War economy measure vast numbers were recoated for use again, and in the 1930s there are tales of wheelbarrow-loads being removed for destruction in Liskeard. In Looe, a great many were once used to fill an awkward hole in the floor.

An historic photograph is included here, a calotype that was taken at Mount Edgcumbe by the pioneer Henry Fox Talbot with his small wooden handmade camera in 1845. Probably this is the earliest photograph to be taken in Cornwall. Also there are one or two of the very early photographs taken in Polperro by Lewis Harding in the 1860s. An amateur, using a wet plate camera he created a record of life in the village that at that time was quite unique. His work and even his name became forgotten for many years, only to be rediscovered quite recently.

Each year in the early 1900s Herbert Hughes with a party of friends came down from the Midlands for photographic holidays. Over the years he created a series of studies of seascapes and Cornish harbours of superb quality. Photographs by Hughes taken in Looe and Polperro are included here. One shows him and his friends at work on the Banjo pier at Looe wearing caps and one adventurous boater, thick woollen socks and plus fours; all practical clothes for transporting their heavy cameras and tripods up stony Cornish cliff paths.

All these photographers in their time found their subjects in East Cornwall with the scenery constantly changing in the clear light, its ancient fishing ports and historic inland towns, and the faces of the local people too. Turn the pages to see the record they have left us of what they saw. I hope that their pictures, linked to the varied stories of the past that they evoke, and the details captured in some of the old postcard views may provide for you, as they do for me, a fascinating if fragmented mirror of past times in this part of Cornwall.

LEFT *Fore Street, Liskeard.*

ABOVE Fore Street. Looking towards the clock tower, an early
motor car is parked by the Royal Hotel, while 'Carless Petrol' is
available on the right. Two farmers in bowlers and polished boots
discuss prices outside the cattle market and an elegant gas lamp
serves a boy as a leaning post in front of the Devon and Cornwall
Bank.

ABOVE St Petroc's Church, Bodmin, the stone steps leading from the square towards St Goran's wellhouse and the crenellated porch of the church. Here, in the upper chamber wall, 200 years ago, the beautiful ivory reliquary of St Petroc was found concealed.

Long ago in the sixth century St Goran and later his friend St Petroc settled beside this flowing spring and worked to convert the people of the pagan settlements on the hills around. Close to St Goran's well the first tiny Celtic Christian church was built. Much later, in medieval times, the forty prosperous trade guilds of Bodmin town subscribed to build the present church. It cost them £194 3s 6½d, and asserted their new independence from the rule of old Bodmin Priory in the valley below.

This postcard of the scene in 1904 shows no roundabout or busy stream of cars, and the old gentlemen can take a peaceful stroll.

LEFT On the right is the glass-canopied entrance to the Royal Hotel. Beside Bodmin's old coaching inn is H. Chapman's Billiard Hall with a restaurant upstairs. Next door the Costumier is also agent for Plymouth Dye Works – useful for mourning clothes! On the left of Fore Street the gas lamp advertises the Coffee Tavern, a teetotal answer to the forbidden attractions on the other side of the street.

Dated 10 August 1914, on the back of this postcard a mysterious message reads: 'My country would not accept my Services, so I came out here to beat worries – long woolley ones. Chin, Chin. H.B.'

Perhaps the writer was luckier than he knew...

RIGHT Bodmin Station in 1915, later closed by Beeching's cuts. The GWR built it in 1887 to link with Bodmin Road and the main line to London. The horse and trap with top-hatted driver and a solid-wheeled motor tourer offer rival ways of getting home. Plenty of room to stand around and no obvious Rules of the Road.

LEFT The County Assize Court on the left, scene of many dramatic murder trials, was built on the site of a 'folly', really the forgotten remains of a medieval Friary. When the new foundations were dug, skeletons were found, dusty relics of the old friars' burial ground.

The great cannon still flanking the steps in 1910 were trophies of the Crimean War, later to be melted down to help another War Effort. The graceful fountain, too, has gone, around which the stalls of the weekly market used to stand.

ABOVE The Judge's procession crosses Church Square in 1945.

RIGHT On the Assize Court steps in 1903 waiting for the arrival the Prince and Princess of Wales (later George V and Queen Mary). Bodmin's Mayor is somewhat eclipsed by the feather boas and fine millinery of the leading citizenry. In the background the Honorable Tommy Agar-Robartes surprisingly retains his hat. Alongside him stands his twin sister, the Honorable Everilda Aga Robartes.

RIGHT February 1906 Election Day picture of Tommy Agar-Robartes, eldest son of the family at Lanhydrock House. Dapper with lily of the valley in his buttonhole, he stood as Liberal candidate and won the East Cornwall seat, with a majority of 1172.

Hon. T.C.A. Robartes (Liberal)	5201
Horace B. Grylls (Conservative Unionist)	4029
Majority	1172

FT Robartes only enjoyed his parliamentary seat for a bare three onths. Then political rivals brought a petition to unseat him on June 1906. The case was heard before three judges sitting gether.

Excessive expenses had been paid, it was alleged, to woo ectoral votes: brass bands and torch processions, a free garden rty for 3000 people at Lanhydrock House, and also large youts for voters' railway fares and drinks.

The three judges found against him. Robartes lost his rliamentary seat, a rare event, but not his popularity. Later his ponents were booed up the street. Only a year or so after, bartes became a popular Liberal MP for the St Austell Division.

There was a sad sequel in 1915. As Captain Tommy Agar-bartes MP Coldstream Guards, he was killed at the battle of os. Under heavy fire he carried water to a gravely wounded mrade and was shot himself with an expanding bullet in the ng. For this brave action his fellow MPs recommended him for a sthumous VC, and he was long remembered in Cornwall as a al war hero.

ABOVE Bodmin Gaol when all the buildings were intact. This other great institution in the town was built as a model establishment in the late eighteenth century. To modern thinking the regime was harsh, using treadmills, a punitive gruel diet and overcrowding in underground cells. Public executions continued here until late in the nineteenth century.

High up on the façade of the Women's Wing (on the right) a scaffold would be erected. Offenders against the law of property as well as murderers were publicly hanged, providing a spectacle for citizens ranged along the hillside opposite the gaol. Intended as a deterrent, too often the ceremony became a gruesome entertainment. Special excursion trains brought thousands into Bodmin town, for example, in 1840 when the murderous Lightfoot brothers were despatched in this fashion. Afterwards the audience dispersed to carouse in local inns and to patronise lurid reconstructions of the crime, staged in dingy fairground booths.

LOW The murder site at Pencarrow Mill. On 8 February 1840, a
murky night, Mr Nevell Norway was riding home from Bodmin to
Wadebridge along the turnpike. Just at this spot near the mill at
9 p.m. he was brutally attacked by the two Lightfoot brothers
who lay there concealed, intending to rob. Twice they fired a
pistol that failed to go off and so resorted to battering their
victim's head with the butt. Desperate to hide the robbed and
bloody corpse they dragged it across the road and half into a
stream by the cottage on the left. The brothers made their escape
but being known locally as suspicious characters they were quickly
apprehended, tried and publicly executed at Bodmin, the event a
general holiday.

A mysterious sequel occurred when Edmund, the victim's
brother, was returning from a long sea voyage. He was captain of
the *Orient* sailing from Manila to Cadiz. On 8 February, the very
night of the murder, going off watch at 10 p.m. he had a vivid and
horrific dream about his brother. It included all the details of the
attack; the double failure of the gun to fire, the blows to the head,
the bloodstained body in the stream by the cottage, and the
robbery. Back on watch at 4 a.m. in some distress, Captain Norway
recounted the dream to his Second Officer, Mr Henry Wren, who
recorded the grim details in the ship's log, all the while chaffing
him as a 'superstitious Westcountryman'.

But, when Captain Norway returned to his home, his brother's
sad fate was confirmed. The written and dated record of his dream
presents strong evidence for the existence of telepathy and
clairvoyance.

LEFT Children carrying gas masks in the early weeks of th Second World War.

RIGHT George VI and Queen Elizabeth visit Bodmin in 1950.

ABOVE The Gatehouse of Lanhydrock House built by the first Lord Robartes whose elevation to the peerage cost him an enforced £10,000 – at least twenty times as much today. The Gatehouse has a Renaissance exuberance of style although built in 1638. It had a serious purpose too, garrisoned as a barbican to defend Robartes' grand new house in times of civil war.

In 1987 the obelisks capping the roof were gently lowered to the ground for strengthening, and found to be hardly impaired after three hundred years of Cornish wind and weather.

LOSTWITHIEL

The traceried octagonal spire of St Bartholomew's Church rises
above the town. The grid pattern of the streets around was laid
out in medieval times after a disastrous fire. Even today, flanking
the alleyways that intersect the streets, the narrow garden plots
are defined by high irregular walls of mingled handmade brick,
grey slate and rosy sandstone. Together with the occasional
pointed arch framing a discreet garden door, these are the only
traces left of the important town that grew up in the shelter of the
Duchy Palace.

During the Civil War, cannonballs hurtled destructively over
the town narrowly missing the church. On Druid's Hill and on the
grassy slopes above the winding Fowey River, Roundheads and
Royalists met in several bloody skirmishes.

ABOVE Lostwithiel and Bridge.

ABOVE The Hall of Exchequer and Exchange of the Duchy Palace, built 1272 and still in good repair today. For hundreds of years it housed the Duchy Parliament, and the Stannary Court and Gaol were built alongside it. Once all tin mined in Cornwall was brought here for assaying and dues to be paid. Those tinners found guilty of trading adulterated ingots were severely punished in its gaol.

During the last war the Palace fulfilled a new role, when its basement doors were opened to provide a shelter from air raids for Lostwithiel residents.

ABOVE Lostwithiel's ancient bridge, last rebuilt in the fifteenth century when all subscribers were granted forty days Indulgence from Purgatory. Like its predecessors it crosses the Fowey just where the salt water meets the fresh coming down from Bodmin moor.

Once a chapel for travellers' prayers stood on this north side and beneath the street a long arched causeway was found, built when the river was much wider and deeper and Lostwithiel the chief medieval port in the county. Only the build up of silt from tin workings upstream put an end to its busy trade.

Behind the boys dangling their feet over the parapet can be seen the chimney of Silver Vein mine. On the far bank was Gooseytown, a notorious ramshackle settlement of the river's bargees.

Nathaniel Coulson, a local workhouse orphan, emigrated and made a fortune as a dentist to the Gold Rush miners of San Francisco. The bells of Grace Cathedral there reminded him of the sweet sound of the church bells in his native town and he sent back £500 to pay for a park for Lostwithiel boys to play in. Laid out along this bank of the river, it is still there today.

LEFT The Old Malthouse on the corner of Taprell Lane and North Street. How many passersby notice this old carved stone? In 1658 the Taprell brothers rented this house for 12 shillings a quarter and lent their name to the lane. As a landlord Walter Kendall was an optimist: his lease still has 2671 years to run: 'Walter Kendal of Lostwithiell was funder of this house in 1658. He hath lease for three thousand yeares which had begining the 29th of September anno 1652.'

RIGHT Queen Street once called Market Street. Lostwithiel Market took place once a month and was held in this street. Cattle roamed freely and farmers leisurely discussed prices opposite the Methodist Church still under construction. All other traffic took to the byways. In 1899 pantechnicons and traffic-light queues were still a nightmare of the future.

ABOVE Parade Square – in front of the Monmouth Hotel in 1915.
The Recruiting March of A Company 13 Battalion Sherwood
Foresters with Captain (later Sir) Robert Howe on the right.

The message on the back of this Dalby Smith postcard reads: '1st
May 1915. Dear Chum, I may have a chance to see you before
going across the water. Can you find your humble on this photo?
This life just suits me – better than the Bank. Hope all the boys
are well remember me to them all. J.R.G. 13841 Lance Corporal
J.R. Gordon.'

RIGHT Ivy-covered Restormel Castle in the 1900s. ' . . . a fine piece
of ruin in fine preservation though very ancient' wrote an early
eighteenth-century tourist.
    But oblivious of the past the young children of Lostwithiel are
gathered here for the annual Methodist Sunday School Treat.
Even the youngest baby sports a wide-brimmed hat and all are
tidy in their Sunday best.

LEFT Lostwithiel Firemen form the Guard of Honour at the wedding of Miss Myrtle Tearle sometime in the 1930s. They are photographed in St Bartholomew's churchyard with Mr Tearle, the bride's father and the leader of the Firemen, beaming his pride and pleasure.

ABOVE Queen Elizabeth and Prince Philip in Lostwithiel in 1962.

RIGHT *Isambard Kingdom Brunel,* one of the last of the great steam engines on the Penzance to Plymouth run, pictured on a rainy day at Lostwithiel Station in the 1960s.

LEFT Line up of the East Cornwall Milk Company lorries outside the depot in the early '30s. There was no dryer tower then to dwarf the ancient buildings of the town.

ABOVE & ABOVE RIGHT Golant in the 1900s, a small harbour on the
River Fowey, boating and fishing its main trade but known for its
plum trees and apple orchards, too. Pictured here is the New Inn
and on the yellow sand of the river bed beyond, revealed at low
tide, the Cornish Good Friday ceremony of 'trigging' for cockles
with bucket and spade continues to take place today.

RIGHT Edwardian ladies on holiday stroll over Lerryn bridge in
1910. It was a favourite destination then as now for boat trips from
Fowey, but a close eye has to be kept on the tide.

BELOW View of Fowey in the 1900s photographed from across the river.

ABOVE A last-century view of Town Quay, Fowey, taken from the
Royal Yacht *Osborne* moored in the river.

LEFT Fowey harbour in 1901. At the mooring place two- and three-
masted schooners wait to load a cargo. A keen eye can pick out
details of their cobweb of rigging, Fowey waterfront and life on
deck.

BOVE Place, the home of the Treffry family for over 700 years. In
13 the house pictured here was partly ruinous and its new
wner J.T Treffry undertook rebuilding and repair. When the
undations of his new tower were dug skeletons were discovered
venty feet down amid traces of chain mail and molten lead from
e roof. These were the last relics of a brave defence of Place
gainst medieval French attackers by Elizabeth Treffry, that saved
e people of the town who had taken refuge there.

The carved Elizabethan oriel, with the Paradise Chamber
stairs, Treffry left unchanged, but to the right of the front door
s Cornish stonecarvers built the large new bay. Sadly, some less-
an-honest workmen caused many delays, risking their own
fety to pay for drink. The scaffolding needed to complete the job
as secretly sold for cash, and the same persistence that created
reffry's industrial empire was required to complete the
construction of Place.

FT The Lugger in Fore Street, a building that has greatly
anged today, but on this postcard it clearly shows its early
igins. George Varco, the landlord looks the part standing
oudly on the threshold in his high-crowned bowler. The camera
s attracted a bevy of young Fowey residents in high, buttoned
ots.

RIGHT Inside an old Fowey house of similar age. Ships' timbers re-used, shaped with an adze, and the stone of the walls showing the pressures of time. The mangle is a sturdy monument to a more recent hardworking past.

LEFT Market Street in 1890, looking towards St Fimbarrus' Church, 'the saint with shining hair'. The cobbled street slopes to the central gutter that carries all debris in the direction of the harbour. On the left the Pure Soda Water Co. (J.M. Williams, agent, The Ship Hotel) does not look like a very prosperous concern.

LEFT 'Noah's Ark' photographed on a snowy day at Christmas time. It is one of the oldest buildings in Fowey, a prosperous merchant's house of Elizabethan times. At one side a passage led to a public well used by the people of the town.

OVERLEAF A panoramic view of Polruan from Fowey in 1900, for centuries the home of shipbuilders, master mariners and salmon seiners, its harbour thought by some to have existed in Roman times, earlier than that of Fowey itself.

At the left of the quay is the shipwrights' yard with a small wet dock for repairs. From Polruan castle in earlier times at sunset a chain was ferried across the river to the blockhouse on the Fowey bank. It was an effective defence against rival pirates and foreign marauders seeking revenge.

On the top of Pencarrow Hill stands Polruan School, later destroyed by a daylight bomb in the Second World War. Nearby, the ruins of St Saviour's Chapel are still a daymark for sailors today, though the medieval pilgrims for whose prayers it was built no longer take ship for Spain from the little port below.

RIGHT Two prominent citizens of Fowey meet in Fore Street. Plus-fours are de rigueur in the 1930s. Sir Arthur Quiller Couch, the town's famous novelist, on the left, and Graham Gullick, local chemist and photographer of Fowey sailing ships, who greets him, on the right.

RIGHT This musical pair earned a precarious living touring Fowey pubs. The lady distributed little bags of lavender and, when she sang, pennies were quickly donated as encouragement to move on

ᴏᴠᴇ Outside the Commercial Hotel the Treffry coachman halts
s gleaming well-groomed horses. The landlord of the
ᴏmmercial, John Martin, had less panâche. He was tried for
iving at over 4 m.p.h. when competing with John Frost of The
ʜip to collect customers from Lostwithiel town. A further fall
ᴏm grace that occurred when he was arrested drunk at the
ilway station there, led to the Commercial's rackety reputation.
ᴏday it has become the Safe Harbour and times have changed.

RIGHT Once Bodinnick Hill was on the only southern route into Cornwall and many a weary traveller's horse stumbled in the muddy ruts of this steep descent to the ferry crossing to Fowey and beyond.

Pictured in 1901 the long sweeps of the ferry can be seen behind Butson's boatyard wall. The old house opposite is the *Ferryboat Inn* also kept by this family. Beer supplies were brought up using the donkey and dray and little Edie Butson out playing with her brother is perplexed by the black hood of the camera.

If your name's Butson you can build boats.' In this small yard at Ferryside, then called Swiss Cottage, prior to the 1880s, many deep-water schooners were built by the Butson family, using a wooden frame on the narrow strand: *Gallant* and *Undine, Thetis, Rippling Wave* and *Gem* and many more. Some sailed as West Indiamen in the fruit trade, and made record passages, but as sail gave way to steam for deep water voyages, local ship builders had to concentrate on smaller craft. In a pre-fibreglass age they built wooden boats with the old skills handed down from Norse times. When in the 1900s this yard finally closed, Cecil, one of the ten brothers, went out to Ontario and founded a Butson ship repair yard that flourishes today.

LEFT Joe and Percy Butson with Edie, from the family of ten boys and one girl, with two newly built dinghies in the yard.

RIGHT Harold and John Butson with a dinghy and a light racing skiff.

ABOVE St Neot Bridge across the Loveny river. Over this little
bridge in earlier times went all the traffic between Bodmin and
Liskeard. Travellers on horseback, packponies loaded with tin,
bespattered pedestrians and an occasional lumbering wagon, all
were prepared for sudden floods and precipitous hills and
potholes.

Later the *Carlyon Arms* or 'Club' was built to serve the
St Neot tin trade. It remained an inn till the 1920s but is now a
friendly petrol station. Up the valley behind it can be found
St Neot's ancient well and, in the garden of the house next door, a
stone tin-ingot mould was unearthed, now set in the wall as mute
evidence of a once thriving trade.

BELOW Barras Street, Liskeard (once Barrel Street) looking towards the Parade. An early motor passes on the 'wrong' side of the street. The dog strolls in the road and there is not much to recall the visit of Charles I to slate-hung Stuart House on the right, when he slept there for several nights during his Civil War campaigns in the West. Today Stuart House stands empty and forlorn and a local Trust seeks support to bring life back to it again.

RIGHT The Parade has always been the heart of the town. For centuries the Bull Post stood here, a large stone with a stout iron ring set in it. The mayoral budget (accounts) included a regular item – '2d for a rope to beat (bait) the bull' – and even on occasion a badger or bear. Small dogs when tossed were caught in the women's aprons as they stood by. Later bets would be laid on 'cockfights as usual' held in the many town inns. Only during Victoria's reign did the literary and scientific societies of Liskeard supplant the cruder entertainments of earlier times.

LEFT At the far end of Barras Street facing towards the Parade
here once stood elegant Trehawke House. Known as Trehawke
the Miser's house it was originally built in the eighteenth century
with a prominent turret. Regular deliveries of smuggled brandy
and other goods were arranged by the miserly Trehawke and
stowed in this house's capacious cellars. Some spoke of secret
passages into the town, and his servants were terrorised into
silence when he played an eerie violin below their attic sleeping
quarters. The erratic sounds heard in the small hours discouraged
curiosity or gossip.

Later a more decorous regime prevailed. John Allen, the
Liskeard historian, lived here with his wife and four daughters
who all wore strict Quaker dress. Pictured here with his wife in a
bath chair they are to be seen in the quiet garden that long ago
disappeared under the concrete pavements of the cattle market.
Trehawke House was demolished and in time replaced by the
National Westminster Bank, also with a turret today.

LEFT The four springs feeding the Pipe Well have never been known to fail. This plentiful supply served the Celtic chieftain wh built his castle on the hill above it, and later a medieval royal palace and the town that grew up around it. So the date on the Victorian gate is deceptive. Much earlier, mayoral rules for the us of this well were strict. A nearby notice read: 'Bellies must not be washed in this well – people of the lower sort must use the lower trough.'

BELOW Market Street in the 1920s where an early tourist could find a postcard or china souvenir at Ferries' the printer. Up the street on the same side the curved front of the Market House has an advertisement for the Pickles Electric Cinema upstairs. Liskeard Market in earlier times brought profits to the residents but also riotous scenes. Rules for decorous behaviour were drawn up: no arguing in the street, and no scolding or malicious gossip permitted.

Liskeard Market Day.

"BANANAS, all ripe, two and three a penny."—"Who'll have a large Hake for 1½d.?"—"Boot Laces, one penny buys another half-dozen, half-a-dozen for a penny." "Here you are, mum, a yard of Tripe for 1½d."—"All the latest Songs: Stop yer tickling, Jock; There's work in the Workhouse yet."—"Oranges all sweet, some of 'em."—"I say, here's a beauty, a nice young Rabbit for 9d."—"Well, my dear, what be 'ee going to have?"—"Any old Rags, Bones, or Rabbit Skins."—"Beautiful Honey, did 'ee want a quart?" "Onions! very sheep to-day, very sheep."—"Fresh Water Cresses."—"Sold out, Bill?" "No; I 'aint took enough for the lodgings yet." "Are we down hearted?" "No!"—Police: "Move on! Move on!")

LEFT Itinerant basket sellers in 1908 display their wares. Good custom was certain before the age of the plastic bag and deliveries were made by the boy with the specially designed wheelbarrow. The imposing Wesleyan Chapel up the street had a predecessor that stood for a mere four years before it was destroyed by malicious arson and the culprit was only revealed by his own deathbed confession.

LEFT A striped pole advertises the barber's one-roomed shop at the top of the stone steps. Next door is the Ancient House, still there today, its exact age forgotten but betrayed by its rugged stone pillared porch.

Along Church Street in the 1840s a riot flared. It started outside the Buller Arms when 200 tinners were denied more beer. Mining was thirsty work and men and times were hard.

ABOVE John Davey's Engineering Works in 1896. The boss surveys
the scene, bowler-hatted, in the upstairs doorway. The babe in
arms is Arthur Moyse who in later life managed Sweet's Yard
during the 1950s. But here horses have not yet been ousted by
machines.

ABOVE RIGHT The Queen and Prince Philip at Liskeard in the
1950s escorted by the Mayor, Mr Arthur Snell, with a crowd of
loyal citizens. Among those present were Douglas Marshall,
Sir Edward Bolitho, Mr and Mrs Tank, and Macebearer Mr Moon.

RIGHT A summer tea party in the garden of the small house in
Lower Lux Street where John Henry Coath, the Liskeard
photographer, opened his first studio in the town. Hilda Coath,
Mrs Lashbrook and Miss Doris May.

ABOVE Phoenix United, the mines on the south west slope of
Caradon Hill, brought work and prosperity to Liskeard town and
to places around. In their heyday £315,000 profit was made from
copper dug out there. Many a fortune was made by the mines'
Adventurers, but not by the eighty men and eighty women who
laboured to raise the ore. Wages were low and conditions tough.
At South Phoenix young boys employed in buddling the ore asked
for a raise to 2s. 6d. a week but were summarily refused.

BELOW Bottom of an engine shaft.

ABOVE Long before the mining boom Daniel Gumb housed his family here on the rocky hillside below the Cheesewring. Stonecarving was his unprofitable trade but his enthusiasm was for mathematics. On the great boulder roofing his 'house' can still be seen his carved diagram illustrating the 47th proposition of Euclid – 'The square on the hypotenuse of a right-angled triangle is equal to the sum of the squares on the other two sides.'

By the entrance to his humble home Daniel Gumb inscribed his name and date but an example of his professional work is a memorial he carved on the outside wall of Linkinhorne Church:

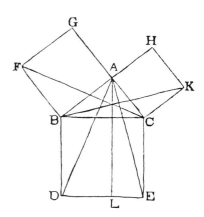

> *Here we lye without the wall*
> *T'was full within we made a brawl*
> *Here we lye no rent to pay*
> *And yet we lye so warm as they.*

ABOVE Morval House the ancestral home of the Buller family. The impressive mullioned façade, the oak panelling and unique carved wood staircase within record the long prosperity of this family as property owning squires in East Cornwall. In the more brutal times of the Wars of the Roses, John Glynn who owned the earlier house on this site, was lured outside at 4 a.m., ambushed, robbed and torn limb from limb by political rivals from Liskeard. Not trusting local justice in such desperate times his wife sought redress from a Cornish jury that sat in London.

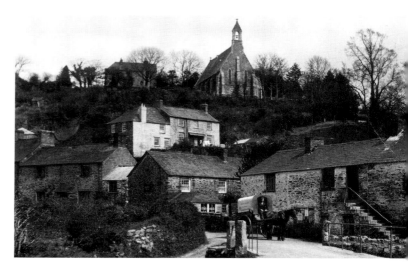

ABOVE St Keyne's Well in the East Looe Valley. Mrs Sambles of
the cottage nearby takes her pitcher to the well. Did she profit by
the special power of the Saint's holy waters to confer authority in
marriage to the first of a couple to drink?

The Quality that Man or Wife
Whome Chance or Choice attains
First of the sacred spring to drink
Thereby the Mastery gains.

R. Carew 1602

RIGHT Four streams and several old roads meet in this remote
village at Herodsfoot at the foot of wooded hills west of Liskeard.
On one of the distant slopes stood the East Cornwall Gunpowder
Mill seeking the dampness of the trees around for extra safety.
The Mill's long history of supplying the local mines and quarries
was sadly ended by a fatal explosion in 1963. The following year
its long guarded secret formula was sold to ICI.

ABOVE Looe station photographed in 1880 when the railway track continued on past the bridge to the quays. There were passengers then but the main freight was blocks of granite from Cheesewring quarry and copper ore from Caradon mines. Piled on Buller quay it awaited shipment to distant parts loaded on to the schooners moored alongside.

RIGHT Liskeard and Looe Railway: station staff in 1910. Are the boys extra young employees or pioneer train spotters? The engine is either *Looe* or *Lady Margaret*.

LEFT Across the river is the old Bone Mill, a tide mill built in 1614 to grind corn, but later bones for fertiliser. The tide at flood in the river was caught within the millpool wall and as it ebbed the imprisoned sea water was slowly released through the narrow sluices under the mill. The force of its escape turned the heavy granite grinding stones. Today only a fragment of the millpool wall remains around the boating pool, and the old mill itself long ago ceased its work and is now a tourist café.

ABOVE A 1920's postcard of East and West Looe looking upriver. Behind the tall warehouses and fishlofts lining the quay are the sturdy old chimneys and huddled slate roofs of medieval East Looe. One solitary truck stands on the railway track and, beyond the special crane for shifting the granite blocks, there are only three cars and one lonely charabanc parked on Buller Quay.

In rival West Looe the old range of coastguard cottages built to discourage smuggling are flanked by hotels and board residences for the new tourist trade. The older houses of the town crowd closer to the quay.

RIGHT East Looe Fish Market: the dogfish catch.

ABOVE *Our Daddy*, a well-known local fishing boat built in the shipyard beside the bridge in West Looe and owned by the Pengelly family for over sixty years.

ABOVE Cleaning pilchards in 1890 – a messy job requiring plenty
of water, an accurate knife and nimble hands, the hard-working
fingers sometimes protected with bits of rag.

ABOVE The schooner *Priscilla* in Looe River, 1904.

RIGHT Even in more recent times a woman's work is never done.

ABOVE *Little Dorrit* moored beside St Nicholas' Church in 1880.
She was known for her seaworthiness despite her small tonnage,
and had made deep-water voyages all the way to Newfoundland,
where her small size was an asset in picking up salt cod cargoes
from shallow harbours and narrow inlets. The fish she carried to
Italy or Spain, and then brought home cargoes of salt. Here she is
engaged in the coasting trade.

BELOW A Hughes photograph of the fourteenth-century church of
St Nicholas, West Looe. For nearly 200 years this building was
secularised as the town's Guildhall and at different times it has
housed a theatre, a school, a market, a prison and a large scold's
cage. The latter could hold more than one nagging or troublesome
female at a time and the names of those so punished were
carefully recorded. No man seems to have been punished in this
way.

ABOVE Looe Beach in 1920, with no bathing costumes to be seen but plenty of hats, essential wear when out of doors. The row of changing tents were preceded by a lone wooden bathing machine, prematurely installed on this beach in 1800, one of the first in the country, but by 1820 it had disintegrated through lack of use.

BELOW Luggers leaving harbour on the evening tide.

ABOVE An earlier beach party photographed in 1910. Perched on
the rock the bored young lady in a motoring hat and veil seems to
regret the outing. Note the large box camera on the sand.

RIGHT The wreck of the *Marguerite,* a Boulogne trawler, stuck fast on the rocks of Talland Bay after running ashore in a dense fog in 1922. The crew was rescued by Looe lifeboat and children have walked over from there, and from Polperro too, to see the thrilling spectacle, photographed by A.E. Raddy.

LEFT The May Garland Fair at Lanreath where a maypole was decorated with a garland of hawthorn, a fertility symbol, instead of the usual ribbons. Invaders from neighbouring villages often planned the theft of the pole so a close guard was mounted by the men of Lanreath. But here the younger folk have no such responsibilities.

ABOVE Talland Church. Tucked under the brow of the hill above Talland Sands this ancient church has been the scene of many dramas in its time. One of its vicars in early Georgian times, the Reverend Richard Doidge, was renowned through the neighbouring countryside as a successful exorcist. At dusk he could be seen in black coat and periwig whipping an unruly horde of ghosts past the church, down the steep hill to the sea. Stories of hauntings helped the smugglers of these parts and courage was lacking to investigate the secret runs of contraband concealed amongst the gravestones of this lonely churchyard.

In 1812 Reverend Whitmore, a curate here, absconded with the church funds, was later proved an impostor and a forger, and ended his life on Gloucester gallows. Those joined by him in this church in matrimony had uncomfortable doubts about the legality of their unions.

ABOVE Polperro in 1904 when the pilchard shoals had begun to desert these waters. The crews of the small 'gaffers' moored snugly behind the net-hung pier worked hard to gain a living.

On the steep sides of the serpentine valley behind the harbour their stone and cob cottages cling in higgledy piggledy order. Within some of the thick stone walls can still be found the hideouts and concealed passageways once used to evade the press-gangs. In those earlier days a precarious existence could be eased by local skills at privateering and the contraband trade. The only road into the village then was down 1 in 3 Talland Hill and the law was seldom enforced.

OVERLEAF A Raddy photograph of the harbour Fish Market.
Weighing the fish with Ned Middleton, the Buyer from Looe,
appraising the conger catch.

ABOVE In 1860 a visiting artist has set up his easel in front of the *Three Pilchards* inn. This hostelry resisted several petitions for its closure by a strong Temperance movement in the village, and survives triumphantly today.

This rare early photograph was taken by Lewis Harding, an invalid who came to Polperro to convalesce under the care of Doctor Jonathan Couch. He occupied his father's cottage in the village and lived there many years. With ample time on his hands he devoted it to mastering the new art of photography. But the steep hills around and the 100 pounds weight of equipment required for the wet plate process he used, kept him very close to home. So he created a photographic record of the life of the village and its people, making atmospheric studies of the harbour and streets and a series of individual portraits unique at that time.

The fishermen and their families got to know him well and tolerantly accepted the occasional requirement to remain motionless for minutes at a time in front of his camera. Harding's instructions to the young lads (RIGHT): they are not to move or to look directly at the lens to avoid recording a startled blink, or worse, a blur. When he died, Harding's name and pioneer work became quite forgotten. It is only quite recently that the photographs he took have been discovered again, their fine and historic qualities appreciated, and his identity revealed by some clever detective work.

RIGHT In the Warren in 1890. Donkeys roamed freely around the village and carried many a load of sand or fish in dorsels on their backs. A Polperro woman always had knitting to do, a guernsey for her fisherman husband, or socks to sell to earn a few pence. The little girls learnt the art very young and played all their games with knitting pins tucked firmly under one arm.

RIGHT Men at work resurfacing the street with cobbles from a nearby beach, with the aid of a Cornish wheelbarrow and a Cornish spade.

wo old post card views of Polperro. On the right the caption
ads: 'A promising recruit.'

ABOVE Polperro post office in 1902 – Alfred Ernest Raddy is the young man waiting with the post van. In it was a locked box for valuables and a gun for defence. Every day at 6 a.m. he had to collect the mail from Liskeard station and bring it on a tortuous route via St Keyne, Duloe, Sandplace, Looe and on to Polperro. The clatter of his pony's hooves served as an alarm clock for the people in the cottages he passed.

The six mile journey back was not till 5 p.m. Bored with this long daily wait, Raddy tried his hand around the village with a bellows camera and tripod. Since he knew Polperro people well he was not short of subjects and the many fine photographs he took of village life at that time reveal his talent for composition and a natural photographic skill. Luckily most of his fragile glass negatives survive today.

His hobby became a profession and his first studio was in Polperro – a painted backcloth set up against a cottage wall, with his subjects posed in front of it on the cobbles of the street.

When he got married Raddy moved his family and his studio to Looe. In the years to come he took a series of unique photographs of the town and harbour there, many included in this book. His son Tom became a professional photographer, too, and in the rambling Elizabethan house in Looe's Fore Street where A.E. Raddy first established his studio, the business continues today in the hands of Rex Raddy and his son, the third and fourth generation of this photographic family.

RIGHT Polperro harbour with waiting donkey carts in just the right position to carry the eye over the water to the boats beyond and the potato patches of the fishermen on the hillside, cultivated to help with winter food shortages. An A.E. Raddy photograph.

ABOVE This little boy with the enviable curls was one of H. E. Raddy's first 'studio' subjects, taken in a Polperro street.

ABOVE Weighing the fish catch on Polperro Quay in 1903 using
the harbour scales, a photograph by A.E. Raddy.

RIGHT Preparing to leave with the evening tide. A Herbert
Hughes photograph taken in 1914.

CALLINGTON

The town perches on the south flank of Kit Hill, which commands a strategic view over the whole of East Cornwall. Often described by its residents as 'nine miles from everywhere' the town inspires a fierce loyalty all the same.

ABOVE Looking up Fore Street towards Tillie Street with the gas lamp and portico of Golding's Hotel extending over the pavement on the left. The eighteenth-century façade of this old posting inn retained its symmetry in 1910. Today the portico remains but the entrance door is blocked and half of the building has been demolished to provide a new route through to the market.

A 1759 bill for a traveller staying at *New Inn,* Callington (later *Golding's* and then *Blue Cap* hotel) read: Firing 6d, Horses 2/6d, Traveller's Eating 2/8d, Brandy 2d, Cyder 4½d, Ale 3d, Punch 1/3d.

LEFT Launceston Road, Callington, in the 1900s looking toward the centre of the town.

LEFT Launceston Road, Callington, in the 1900s looking toward the centre of the town.

GHT These old houses once ood on the edge of Callington urchyard and their onderous chimneys prompted Victorian disciple of Ruskin make this rare architectural awing. They faced on to llie Street, the most ancient oroughfare of the town and lieved by some to be the site King Arthur's Cornish onghold, his palace of elliwic. Nowadays Tillie Street sadly truncated and only one d house and the former Town ink remain to hint at its busy st.

RIGHT 'Ancient, large strong and fayre' medieval Cotehele, the former home of the Edgcumbe family, hidden among the chestnut woods on the Cornish bank of the Tamar. This crenellated gothic tower was added to the manor house in 1627 by a wealthy Dutch merchant who took refuge here after fleeing from the grip of the Spanish Inquisition. In this remote spot he spent the rest of his life, eventually knighted by James I who had borrowed large sums from him.

RIGHT Arsenic obtained from spent copper mines in the Callington district was much in demand for insecticide in the cottonfields of the American South. Cornish workers handled the deadly substance with only the protection of cottonwool in the nostrils and a triangle of scarf to keep the dust from the mouth. Soap and water were thought to be efficacious, too, but sadly 83 per cent of these miners died young of respiratory disease.

ABOVE In the little chapel with a quaint bellcote was the family
vault where in 1666 Colonel Piers Edgcumbe buried his young
wife Mary after a brief illness. But the rascally sexton, knowing
the value of the rings on her hand, stealthily opened the tomb the
same night under cover of dark. As the uncertain light from his
horn lantern revealed the young woman's body he saw it sigh and
stir. Slowly she recovered from her deathlike trance and the
sexton fled never to be seen again. In her thin shroud Mary beat
on her husband's door. After her grim experience she lived on for
many more years and eventually bore her husband another child.

ABOVE Busy Calstock shown on a postcard of the 1890s. *SS Albion* is at the quay loading granite from quarries nearby. The great Calstock railway viaduct over the river has not yet been built. Out in midstream a paddleboat crowded with passengers ferries them back from a day at Devonport Market and one of the Tamar sailing barges, so numerous then, tacks skilfully upstream with the tide.

SALTASH

BELOW At Saltash Passage fishwives and children, gaily uniformed soldiers and some gentlefolk, too, crowd the small ferry boats for a passage over the Tamar to Saltash town. With their long sweeps and little room to manoeuvre, the ferrymen have a hard task. Out in midstream they will row past the great wooden warships moored there for shelter against surprise French attack. J.M.W. Turner drew this crowded scene of Napoleonic times during his Westcountry tour of 1812.

LEFT In 1917 much larger pleasure steamers are moored here allowing day trippers from Plymouth a pleasant visit to Calstock for tea. For the return journey the steamers also loaded produce grown for market on the sun-facing slopes above the Tamar: strawberries and apples, damsons and pears. A longer trip from Calstock on a steam packet to London was possible too.

RIGHT This unique photograph was taken in 1864 from scaffolding above Saltash Station showing Brunel's Royal Albert Bridge only five years after it was opened. The engine, train and rail are still broad gauge, and ladies on the platform in wide-skirted crinolines with their escorts in stovepipe hats also betray the early date of this view.

ABOVE Mary Ann Pope's cockle shop in Tamar Street, Waterside, Poke Lane in Drake's time, and later known to Devonport sailors as Picklecockle Alley. Annie was sought out for the shellfish she sold; cockles and oysters, mussels, crabs and shrimps. These she simmered and stirred with a red hot poker making them a mouth-watering pink. Her supplies came from the clear tidal waters of the Tamar, quite unpolluted then.

The Tudor doorway to her house is dated 1584 and perhaps it had a grander owner once. Today the house is gone but the dated lintel still survives, re-erected somewhere else in the town – the arch the wrong way round.

LEFT Some of these old houses on Saltash's Waterside dated back to Tudor times. Drake and Hawkins and their men knew these streets when they sought the shelter of the river for their ships. Henry Martin painted this street, Lower Middle Street, in 1899 when many of the houses had smugglers' former hideouts or cellar ladders to a concealed underground passage to the beach.

ABOVE Just past Herbert Simon's grocery shop on the corner of Fore Street, the milkman halts his cart to fill a lady's jug with fresh milk straight from the churn. Across the muddy street is the Railway Hotel lit by a solitary gas lamp. A bomb fell on the corner shop during a war-time raid and now there is just an empty space.

RIGHT A fair at Waterside in 1905 with the steam roundabout set up outside Bennett's Union Inn and a row of wooden swingboats well patronised by the sailors and their young ladies. Once cockfights were staged on this beach and the six-oared cutter in the foreground is a reminder of the age-old skills of Saltash men, and women too, as oarsmen making use of the tides in the river.

RIGHT A slightly more genteel meeting place – Newbury's Rustic Tea Garden situated near the Old Ferry Road in Saltash.

ABOVE This early print shows the first Port Eliot, the original house built near the church by John Eliot from the ruins of the great Cornish priory that once stood here. Walled gardens slope down to the river retaining a trace of the old monastic order.

In medieval times the monks here were once excommunicated, cursed with bell, book and candle by their bishop, who denounced them as 'certain satellites of Satan'.

RIGHT Antony Passage Tea Gardens

ABOVE Monday, and washday at St Germans' Almshouses,
maintained by the Eliot family to house poor widows. The young
girl in a snow-white ankle-length apron leans on her sit-up-and-beg
bike to chat to a busy resident.

ABOVE Antony House in the late afternoon, its classical granite façade softened by the slanting light, with the rosy brick colonnaded pavilions built on each side of the court. Antony, or 'place of apples', has been the Carew family home for over 400 years (now the Carew-Poles).

In the grounds by the Lynher River is a unique early eighteenth-century bath house, supplied twice daily with fresh tidal water from the river flowing up a stone-lined channel.

Much more remote, in woodland above a small creek, is the site, lost now even to memory, of the old house, the home of Richard Carew the Elizabethan poet, whose *Survey of Cornwall* is so dear to its readers. But there are traces still of his 'fishfull pond', the tidal pool fed with sluices that he constructed to house his fish, on whose banks he found repose and delight. In his pocket when he died was found a paper with these lines:

Full thirteen fives of years I toyling have o'repast
And in the fowerteenth weary entred am at last.
While Rocks, Sands Storms & leaks, to take my bark away
By greif, troubles, sorrows, sicknes did essay,
And yet arriv'd I am not at the port of death,
The port to everlasting Life that openeth,
My time uncertain Lord, long certain cannot be,
Whats's best to mee's unknown: & only known to thee.
O by repentance & amendment grant that I
May still live in thy fear & in thy favour dye.

RIGHT Richard Carew aged 32 in 1586

ABOVE Torpoint, or Tarpoint. Long before the town existed this beach was in use for careening; tarring and cleaning off barnacles from the keels of wooden ships laid up on the sand. This postcard of the 1900s shows two 'wooden walls' still moored out in the Hamoaze, and a variety of younger craft as well.

ᴀʙᴏᴠᴇ The Torpoint 'Benefactor of Mankind' Lodge, a branch of
ᴛʜᴇ *Independent Order of Good Templars.* They used to meet in
ᴛʜᴇir own hall, now the Ambulance hall, and were a Friendly
ᴀociety of varied ages dedicated to mutual self-help. Here they are
ᴩhotographed wearing full regalia in the garden of Salamanca
ᴀouse, the residence of Mr J. Hyslop. Back row centre
ᴀr R. H. Nodder; front row 2nd from left Mr J. Hyslop, 4th from
ᴀft Mr W. Bampfylde, far right Mr Frederic Roberts.

ᴌᴇFT Torpoint Ferry, the 'mechanical steam bridge' with its
ᴀnking chains, known to generations of travellers between
ᴧymouth and the far West.

RIGHT Mount Edgcumbe House in its original Tudor
magnificence. After a private visit here the Admiral of the Spani
Armada secretly earmarked the house as his personal prize of wa
Only total defeat at sea destroyed his plan.

    In our time a Nazi firebomb brought complete devastation a
a smaller replica of the house stands on this site today. The
original house, pictured here, was, to quote Richard Carew,
'builded square with a round turret at each end garetted on the
top, and the hall rising in the midst above the rest, which yielde
a stately sound as you enter the same.'

Once there were forty ships moored here at Millbrook and a
mill ground corn in the valley. The town helped to feed
mouth, supplying fish from the cellars of Cawsand and
wrinkle.

Over the shoulder of the hill on the right can be seen the
nney and roof of the former workhouse where once thirty poor
ons were housed. Victorian values ensured that those reduced
ll fortune were better treated than those impoverished
ough vice or idleness'. But all shared the same diet of cabbage
h, bullock hearts, sheepsheads and plucks, pease pudding, salt
and good bread from the mill. Work began at 6 a.m. and
tinued till 6 at night – spinning, mending and washing, picking
um and knotting rope yarn. A high wall enclosed them and
n punishments were imposed on the lazy and refractory.

BELOW At Polbathic the coach stops outside the Halfway House on the turnpike between Torpoint and Liskeard. For the traveller arriving with a thirst the board on the wall of the inn advertises 'Star Ale – No Sediment'.

T This photograph of September, 1845 is probably the first ever
en in Cornwall. Henry Fox Talbot, an English pioneer in the
w art, was also the brother-in-law of Ernest Augustus, the Earl
Mount Edgcumbe. When invited down on a visit to his sister's
use, Talbot brought his newly-invented camera with him.

The calotype he took shows Mount Edgcumbe Battery, a
ence against the French, looking across the river towards the
yal William Naval Victualling Yard at Stonehouse. The ladies of
e family are seated beside the guns. Unless the day was very
ny they probably held the pose quite still for about five
nutes, essential then to obtain a clear image on the special
ht-sensitised paper in Talbot's wooden box camera. The prints
produced by this method, a salt paper print from a calotype
gative, have a characteristic dreamlike quality not captured by
er photographers.

HT Visitors to the Mount
gcumbe grounds enjoy the
w of Plymouth Hoe and
ke's Island, from the
hteenth-century Folly, whose
orated windows came from
emolished medieval chapel
oss the water.

ABOVE Cawsand, with Kingsand beyond, once rival fishing villages but now joined together. For a long time, with Plymouth as an outlet for smuggled goods, these villages were the headquarters of freetrading along the whole east Cornish coast. The Navy kept good contact, too, with such experienced seamen and the crooked alleys, narrow hidden courts, and cottages built with double exits provided a refuge from the press-gang.

In the Old Ship Inn, a three-storeyed house that still overlooks Cawsand beach, Lord Nelson stayed while his warships were revictualled, moored out in the bay.

Up on the slope of the hill behind can be seen the stark walls, partly covered with ivy, of Cawsand Battery, one of Palmerston's Follies built to deter French attack. Its great guns were only fired twice, and never in anger; very fortunate as each time it happened a profusion of window panes shattered in cottages below and the massive walls of the fort developed gaping cracks.

LEFT A local fishwife, typical of those Cawsand women who used to make regular journeys on foot to Plymouth market, via the Cremyll ferry. In earlier days there were reports that some of these ladies had difficulty getting along, impeded by bladders filled with smuggled brandy and concealed beneath their skirts, or else disguised as unprepossessing babes tucked into their shawls.

RIGHT Haddy's bus on the Cremyll run waits near the fountain outside the Cross Keys (now the Smugglers') Inn. In the 1930s there are no parking restrictions, and traces remain of the square's old cobbled drainage channels sloping haphazardly towards the beach.

ABOVE & LEFT Willcock's Tea House in 1910, installed by an enterprising local farmer using water springs in the cliffs for the tea. Seizing a chance he added striped awnings for shade, swingboats and rides on 'Jerusalems' – long-suffering donkeys, to cater for busloads of Edwardian day trippers from Plymouth.

LEFT Edith Smith, the village washerwoman, collecting a bundle of laundry from Mrs Sambells at the gate of her cottage in the centre of Downderry. The tin jug is a discreet way of receiving payment.

GHT Looe Bay, looking down e coast towards Downderry, hitsand Bay and Rame Head.

105

ABOVE Mrs Coath, with her youngest in her arms, watches her other children with their boat in a Downderry rock-pool. The person missing is her husband, the Liskeard photographer, John Henry Coath, who took this family picture.

Year after year, long before the tourist boom, Coath brought his young family here for holidays by the sea. But he and his camera were never idle, and during these visits he took a whole series of panoramic views of this coast and made many creatively posed studies of local people at their work and his children in holiday play.

Those of the photographs taken then, on glass negatives that have survived the hazards of the years, capture for us now the essence of those far off summer days.

BELOW Near the old stone shed with the straw thatch firmly roped against seaside gales, Hilda Coath and her friend Kitty Pooley sit demurely sidesaddle on their diminutive mount. Little George Coath stands proudly in charge of the rein, with a small holly switch in his hand, just in case.

BELOW Hilda brings a cup of tea to Mr Knight, the flint-knapper or 'stone cracker', hard at work preparing materials for the new road built across Seaton Beach in 1905. Beside him on the pile of rocks are the tools of his trade: a 4 lb hammer, a shovel, and in his hand a smaller hammer for finishing touches. A bushel of worked stones like those on the pile, left for the road men in a basket beside the track, earned him a rather small sum.

ABOVE An early view of Seaton Beach before the tourists came.
Not a house on Looe Hill where there are many now, and only a
rough stony track crossing the beach to the old stone bridge.
Under the marram grass there is plenty of sand, later largely
removed to manufacture blocks, rather unsuccessful in fact
because of their high salt content.

The Coath family took the first wooden chalet, built here on
the hill behind the old lime kiln. Two of the boys standing here,
Charles and Claude, followed their father to become skilled
professional photographers, too. Through the more complicated
years of the '30s and '40s Charles photographed these same scenes
and the changes brought by the motor car, a tourist invasion and
ugly wartime beach defences to the quiet seascapes of his
childhood.

LEFT Collecting mussels from the rocks as the tide recedes at the
end of the day. The Irish limpet pickers at Keveral Beach, Seaton,
walked here each year from Plymouth to spend the summer by the
sea. The beach caves gave shelter and mussels, cockles and
limpets were cooked in old tin kettles for later sale.

ALSO AVAILABLE:

AROUND ST AUSTELL BAY
by Joy Wilson
An exploration in words and old photographs around one of the most beautiful bays in Britain.
'... Joy Wilson's text is as warm and as sympathetic as the lovely old pictures, making this a book which glows with interest, a soft lamplight shedding illumination on an era dimmed by the passing years. It is a beautiful achievement...'
The Western Morning News

GREAT HOUSES OF CORNWALL
by Jean Stubbs
The well-known novelist tours seven National Trust properties.
'... she finds a rich vein of history and human interest...'
The Cornish Guardian

100 YEARS AROUND THE LIZARD
by Jean Stubbs
A beautiful title, relating to a magical region of Cornwall, well illustrated, with text by the distinguished novelist living near Helston.
'... the true flavour of life on the windswept peninsula, past and present ... the strange qualities of the flat landscape, the effects of the elements on people's daily lives and, above all, the contrast of past and present are distilled in the text.'
Cornish Life

SEA STORIES OF CORNWALL
by Ken Duxbury, 48 photographs
'This is a tapestry of true tales', writes the author, 'by no means all of them disasters – which portray something of the spirit, the humour, the tragedy, and the enchantment, that is the lot of we who know the sea.'
'... a good mixture of stories, well told by a man with a close affinity to the sea and ships.'
Geoffrey Underwood
Western Evening Herald

FOWEY – RIVER AND TOWN
by Sarah Foot
An enlarged and updated edition of Following the River Fowey.
'The intricate tapestries of this delightful area is woven together with warm, understanding interviews... buy, beg or borrow it.'
The Cornish Times

DAPHNE du MAURIER COUNTRY
by Martyn Shallcross
A very special look at Cornwall in that the internationally-famous novelist has set important stories here. Explores locations which fired Dame Daphne's imagination. The subject of a Radio Cornwall series, produced by Tamsin Mitchell.
'... Anyone whose appreciation of the beauty of Cornwall has been enhanced by Dame Daphne's writing will enjoy this book – a fitting tribute to a remarkable lady.'
Cornish Life

MY CORNWALL
A personal vision of Cornwall by eleven writers who lived and worked in the county: Daphne du Maurier, Ronald Duncan, James Turner, Angela du Maurier, Jack Clemo, Denys Val Baker, Colin Wilson, C. C. Vyvyan, Arthur Caddick, Michael Williams and Derek Tangye with reproductions of paintings by Margo Maeckelberghe.
'An ambitious collection of chapters.'
The Times, London

FESTIVALS OF CORNWALL
by Douglas Williams
Douglas Williams explores some of the great Cornish occasions in the calendar: Hurling and Gorsedd, Crying the Neck and Marhamchurch Revel, Flora Day at Helston and Obby Oss at Padstow are only some of the events covered in words and photographs.
'Douglas Williams has come up trumps again ... captures the individual character of the county's festivals through his love of Cornwall and all things Cornish.'
The Cornishman

UNKNOWN CORNWALL
by Michael Williams
84 drawings and photographs nearly all especially commissioned for this publication, portraying features of Cornwall rarely seen on the published page.
'... a treasure chest of rich jewels that will surprise many people who pride themselves on a thorough knowledge ...'
Western Evening Herald

WESTCOUNTRY MYSTERIES
introduced by Colin Wilson
A team of authors probe mysterious happenings in Somerset, Devon and Cornwall.
Drawings and photographs all add to the mysterious content.
'A team of authors have joined forces to re-examine and probe various yarns from the puzzling to the tragic.'
James Belsey, Bristol Evening Post

THE MOORS OF CORNWALL
by Michael Williams
Contains 77 photographs and drawings. The first ever publication to incorporate the three main moorland areas of Cornwall.
'... is not only a celebration in words of the Moors and their ancient pagan stones and granite strewn tors but a remarkable collection of photographs and drawings of Penwith, Goss and Bodmin Moors ...'
Sarah Foot, The Editor, Cornish Scene

COASTLINE OF CORNWALL
by Ken Duxbury
Ken Duxbury has spent thirty years sailing the seas of Cornwall, walking its clifftops, exploring its caves and beaches, using its harbour and creeks. Over 100 photographs, 45 in colour.
'... a trip in words and pictures from Hawker's Morwenstow in the north round Land's End and the Lizard to the gentle slopes of Mount Edgcumbe country park.'
The Western Morning News

We shall be pleased to send you our catalogue giving full details of our growing list of titles for Devon, Cornwall, Somerset and Dorset as well as forthcoming publications. If you have difficulty in obtaining our titles, write direct to Bossiney Books, Land's End, St Teath, Bodmin, Cornwall.